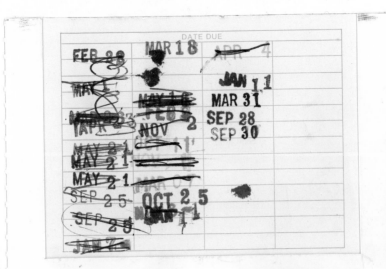

82
78 79 80

HOW SPORTS BEGAN

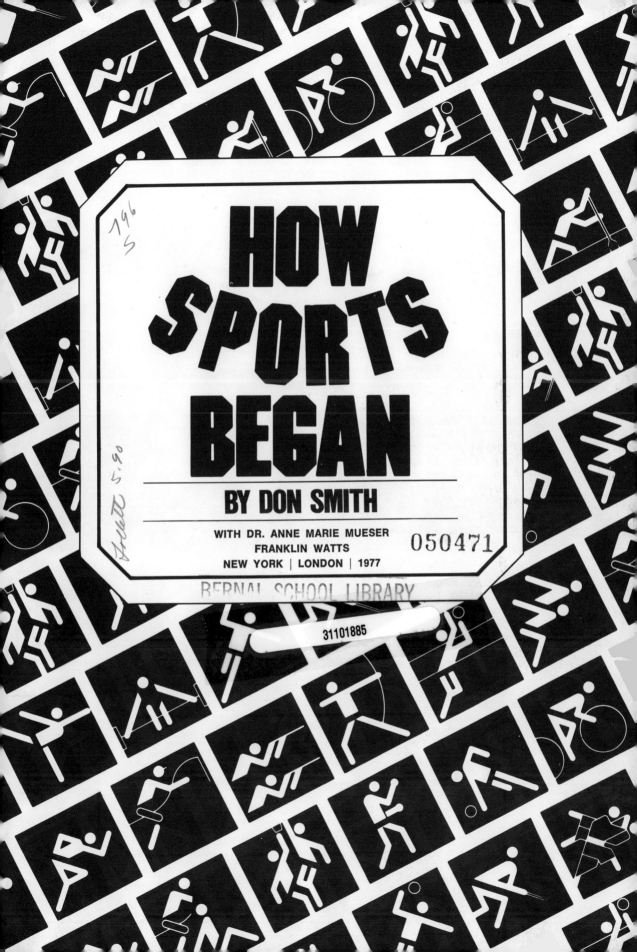

HOW SPORTS BEGAN

BY DON SMITH

WITH DR. ANNE MARIE MUESER
FRANKLIN WATTS
NEW YORK | LONDON | 1977

Photos courtesy of:
Basketball Hall of Fame: pp. 18 (*top* and *bottom*),
21, 22; Museum of the City of New York: pp. 43
(*right*), 75, (The Byron Collection) 50; National
Baseball Hall of Fame & Museum: pp. 4–5, 10
(*top*), 12–13; New York Public Library Picture Collection: pp. 8, 9, 10 (*bottom*), 14, 28–29, 34, 39, 42,
43 (*left*), 46 (*top*), 49, 56, 57, 61, 66 (*top and bottom*),
70, 71, 74 (*top* and *bottom*), 79 (*top* and *bottom*),
85; Pro Football Hall of Fame: p. 35; Public Archives
of Canada: pp. 46 (*bottom*), 53, Japanese Govern-
ment Railways: p. 86.

Library of Congress Cataloging in Publication Data

Smith, Don, 1926–
　　How sports began.

　　Includes index.
　　SUMMARY: Examines legends and facts about
the origins of nineteen popular sports.
　　1. Sports—History—Juvenile literature. [1.
Sports—History] I. Mueser, Anne Marie, joint author.
II. Title.
GV571.S55　　　　　796′.09　　　　76–54143
ISBN 0–531–00093–1

CONTENTS

FOREWORD

In the early days of history, primitive peoples struggled with nature just to stay alive. Huge flesh-eating animals and birds, earthquakes and volcanoes, floods and glaciers were just a few of the terrors constantly facing these early people.

Most sports grew out of the skills that humankind developed in order to stay alive. At first, people ran from the huge beasts that hunted them. Later they learned to throw rocks, kick, and hit—skills useful in hunting as well as in defending themselves against attack. To make food finding easier, many people learned to fish; others developed weapons such as the bow and arrow. Still others learned to swim or row a boat across bodies of water that blocked their path.

Because people were intelligent and aggressive, staying alive gradually became easier. With more free time, people began to use their survival skills for pleasure. By combining a natural love of competition with imagination, people made up games. What a game was like often depended on the geography, weather, equipment available, local customs, space or lack of it, and so on.

The factual histories of the various games and sports played today will be explained in the pages that follow, because they reveal much about our past. We will also look at the stories and legends passed down to us about the various sports. Did Abner Doubleday really invent baseball? Where did ice hockey really begin? Answers to questions like these not only show us the facts, but also tell us a great deal about our culture.

Most games did not start in only one place at one particular time. Nor were most made up by only one person. Similar games were often played in different places at the same time. As people moved around the world, they shared their ideas and changed their games. For example, the ancient Greeks, leaders in many forms of physical fitness, had a type of football game. The ancient Romans adopted the game as part of their military training. It was then brought to the different countries Roman soldiers invaded. When it reached Britain, the game underwent some changes to fit British taste. Eventually, this sport became three separate modern sports—soccer, rugby, and American football.

The purpose of this book is to let you, the curious sports fan, look at the legends and facts concerning many of the various sports played today. Because careful records were so rarely kept, and because one source of information would frequently contradict another, some of the legends and theories presented in the following pages are open to attack. Perhaps new evidence will turn up in the future, and all controversies will be settled. But there is much to be gained even now from a close look at what has come down to us through the years. We think you will be surprised at some of the things you read here. We know you will be entertained.

BASEBALL

If we search for the real beginnings of baseball, we discover that one of sports' most beloved stories—the one of how Abner Doubleday invented baseball—is more fiction than fact.

The legend tells us that Doubleday introduced the game in 1839 in Cooperstown, New York, which is today the home of the Baseball Museum and Hall of Fame.

Various crude forms of ball games had been played before Doubleday's time, but it was Doubleday, the legend goes, who on one warm spring day in 1839, drew the very first diamond-shaped playing field, decided on the number of players for each side, and assigned each player to a position in the field. This "first" baseball game was supposed to have been held in a cow pasture, the one now referred to as Abner Doubleday Field.

What a wonderful story! But, unfortunately, it just does not fit the facts. Doubleday was supposed to have started the game while he was a student at Green's Select School in Cooperstown. But in 1839 Doubleday was a cadet at West Point. In 1837 and 1838 he had been a civil engineer—not a student.

Doubleday went on to become an army officer and a writer. He was never known to talk about baseball or write about it. Then how did his name get linked up with the game?

In 1905, the major leagues appointed a commission to try to determine who invented baseball and where the invention took place. This was thought to be necessary for two reasons: (1) to prove that baseball was truly an American game and not merely an

**Left: the American
game of baseball**

**Below: Abner Doubleday,
1819–1893**

adaptation of some foreign game, and (2) to give the game an official "father" around whose name and memory it could better be promoted. One of the members of this commission, A. G. Mills, had been at the same army post with Abner Doubleday after the Civil War. During the commission's research, Mills came up with a letter from a man named Abner Graves, which went back almost seventy years, and which mentioned that he (Graves) knew for a fact that Abner Doubleday had invented baseball.

Using this letter as its only real evidence, the commission then declared Doubleday the father of baseball. Since Doubleday was born and raised in Cooperstown, New York, it was logical to assume that baseball had first been played there. From baseball's standpoint, Doubleday was an ideal father. He was a native-born American, a West Point graduate, a Civil War hero, and a well-known writer.

Other commissions have since disproved this theory. But even to this day, major league baseball still recognizes Doubleday as the inventor of the game.

Sports historians now believe that modern baseball began somewhere else, many years and many miles from that quiet town in upstate New York. But before we look at how modern baseball began, let's take a look at the game's earliest beginnings.

Some anthropologists claim that batting contests were held in Egypt over five thousand years ago. The ancient Greeks and Romans were also said to have played various games of ball. By the twelfth century, such games found their way into Spain and France. From France they spread to Britain, where a game something more like modern baseball, called stoolball, developed.

In stoolball, a pitcher would throw a crude ball against an upturned stool. The opponent would try to hit or bat the ball away before it reached the stool. In time, a second, third, and fourth stool were added as "bases," to be circled by the batter after hitting the ball. The next rule to be added was that the runner could be "put out" by being hit with the thrown ball. After that the game took on a new name—rounders. It became popular with English schoolchildren fairly quickly.

Modern baseball most likely had its roots in a combination of rounders and another very old game played in Britain and brought to the New World with early British settlers—cricket. Both used a bat, or stick, and a ball. Both had a pitcher, a batter, and a catcher. And in both games, stakes, or bases, between which the batter ran after hitting the ball were set up.

How did colonial cricket change to the early forms of baseball? The bridge may well have been the game of rounders. In rounders, the field was marked by posts or stones. There were no limits to the number of players. Except for the pitcher and batter, players had no special positions on the field. The pitcher was known as the packer, or feeder, and the batter was called the striker. American children probably played rounders with cricket bats and balls. They substituted stakes driven into the ground for the wickets of cricket. The batter, after hitting the ball, could be put out by being hit with the ball thrown by a fielder. Getting someone out this way was called plugging, soaking, or scorching.

As the game of rounders became more popular, the use of cricket gear decreased. Youngsters made their own bats and balls. The balls were often just a piece of wood or a rock wrapped tightly with string. Some were made with wool stocking yarn and strips of old rubber. Bats were made of wood from young hickory or ash trees. They were flat on one side, like cricket bats. Some players may even have walked up to home plate waving a board from a barrel!

Rounders led to several other games, all very much alike. Among the most popular were "One old cat," (or "Two old cat," or whatever), and town ball. "One old cat," like cricket, was a British game. The number of people playing in the game determined the number of bases, and, in turn, the name—"One old cat," "Two old cat," "Three old cat," and so on. Town ball was similar to rounders and "One old cat." It probably came from games played by village youths when there were town meetings.

Gradually, rounders and town ball changed. The stakes, which had often injured players who ran into them, were replaced by flat stones. The stones, in turn, gave way to sacks filled with sand or dirt. The number of players who could take part in a game was also cut down—not to nine, but to a fairly workable twelve or thirteen.

No one knows exactly when the term "baseball" was first used. History does, however, trace similar terms back to at least sixty-one

**Above: mural painting in a
tomb near Beni Hasan, ancient
Egypt, around 1900 B.C.**

**Right: a medieval cricket
match depicted on a
French tapestry of the 1500s**

A. J. Cartwright, 1820–1892

A woodcut of a colonial American baseball game, from *Children's Amusements*, 1820

PLAYING BALL

years before Abner Doubleday is said to have named his invention. A Revolutionary War soldier, in his diary, mentions playing a bat and ball game called "base" at Valley Forge. In 1786, a student at Princeton University wrote about playing a game of "baste ball" on campus. Baseball was referred to even more often after the turn of the century, indicating that the game had definitely changed from rounders, town ball, and "One old cat." Sports historians say that a game known as baseball was played in 1825 at the Round Hill School in Northampton, Massachusetts. At the same time, there were rumors that a baseball club was being formed in Rochester, New York. This club was to have had fifty players, who ranged in age from eighteen to forty. In his 1834 *Book of Sports,* Robin Carver referred to the game as "baseball." He said that baseball was the name "generally acknowledged in our country."

This early form of baseball was a blend of cricket, rounders, and town ball. But it had its own identity and its own roughly drawn set of rules. It was very popular and had a bright future. And, of course, all this was long before 1839, when Abner Doubleday was supposed to have invented the game!

But even though already popular, the game still needed someone to put all the parts together. That someone was Alexander Cartwright, who played the game with the group later to become known as the New York Knickerbockers. Cartwright drew up a set of playing rules, the same ones that form the basis of the game today. He decided on using four bases, including home base, and that they would be set ninety feet apart. Nine players would be on each team, with the two sides being called the ins and the outs. Cartwright determined the exact field positions for the outs, or defensive team, and established a uniform distance between the pitcher and the batter. That distance is almost the same as the one used in softball today.

Cartwright explained his rules one June morning in 1845 to his companions who were playing "Four old cat" on a vacant lot in an area that is now Lexington Avenue and Thirty-fourth Street in New York City. He showed the boys his diagram. They weren't sure it would work, but were willing to try it out. Cartwright had promised them it "would keep everyone playing at once." The boys scratched out the bases in the dirt and began to play.

TURNER.   UMPLEBY.   FORD.   COREY.   R.
        J. R. LINDSLEY.   S. T. BANTHAM.   A. M. COMBS.

KNICKERB

Published by W.

WINNE.   BLISS.   MACDONALD.   GARDNER.   LATHROP.
Captain.
DAVIS.   J. S. HURDIS.   J. C. CUYLER.

KER NINE,

So that is what history tells of how and when the popular game of baseball was born. The young men promptly formed the Knickerbocker Baseball Club and took the game very seriously. Baseball was soon to become famous as "the New York game."

The Knickerbockers were trend-setters. In 1849 they appeared in the game's first official uniforms—handsome straw hats, white flannel shirts, and dark-blue woolen trousers. The style was copied from old cricket uniforms. In 1851, the first box score was kept by a Knickerbocker player during a game with the Washington Baseball Club.

By 1858, twenty-five clubs had banded together in a league. For the first time, all were playing under the same rules. On July 20 of that year, admission was charged for the first time, with enough money collected to pay for the renting of the field. Some 1,500 fans had paid $750—fifty cents each. This was the first hint of pro baseball and the big business to come.

The Cincinnati Red Stockings were baseball's first professional team. They were formed in 1866, but the players only started getting salaries in 1869. Salaries ranged from $600 to $1,400 for an eight-month season. The Red Stockings won sixty-five games in a row during a twelve-thousand-mile road trip. Two hundred thousand fans were on hand to watch. Baseball had truly come of age as a national pastime. That long season, however, was more of a success on the playing field than at the box office. Owners of the team did not get rich. Cincinnati collected $29,726.26, but the expenses came to $29,724.87—which left a profit of $1.39 for the entire season!

Cincinnati introduced knee-length uniforms during its long tour. They were made by a woman named Bertha Bertram, who ran a tailor shop on Elm Street in Cincinnati. She made white knickers, white flannel shirts, and bright red stockings. That's how the team got its nickname.

More modernizations of baseball took place in the 1870s. To cut down on the number of home runs, for instance, the "dead ball," which lacked bounce and was harder to hit as far, was introduced. Also, gloves and catchers' masks began to appear around this time. Before, many players had probably wanted to wear them, but no one wanted to be the first. Some had worn flesh-tinted gloves that could not easily be seen by fans or rivals. Then, in the mid-1870s, A. G.

Spaulding, a famous player of the time, wore a glove in public. The glove was dark brown and everyone could see it. Spaulding even added a little padding to the inside to protect his palm. Most players followed his lead immediately.

James Tyng, a Harvard player, was the first catcher to wear a mask when he was behind the plate. He appeared against Yale one day wearing a fencer's mask that had been adapted for baseball. Though he took a ribbing from the Yalies, within two years every catcher in the major leagues was wearing a mask.

Modern-day baseball players are not embarrassed to think of safety first. The game has come a long way from the time when a player had to catch a line drive bare-handed.

BASKETBALL

There's no mystery about basketball. We know who invented it, when, and why. We also know that basketball, like volleyball, did not evolve from any ancient game played in Egypt or Europe. It began in the United States.

A few people have suggested that basketball can be traced back to ancient Mexico. The Aztec Indians had a game in which they tried to put a stone through a metal ring. However, in that game, the players were not allowed to touch the stone with their hands. They had to put it through the ring with another part of their body. Can you imagine playing basketball without hands?

Basketball was created to fill a need. In the late nineteenth century, leaders of the Young Men's Christian Association (the YMCA) noticed a lack of interest in the organization's physical training program. Membership and attendance were down. Adult members, whose money supported the Y, seemed bored with the activities, which included gymnastics, tumbling, and exercises with dumbbells. These were the only body-conditioning activities recommended to men in their late thirties and forties. Football, soccer, and rugby were too rough. Youthful members of the Y were restless, too. They were looking for new challenges. Clearly, something had to be done.

In the winter of 1891, Dr. Arthur Gulick, superintendent of the physical training department at the Y Training School in Springfield, Massachusetts, took the problem to Dr. James Naismith, one of the

Left: Dr. James Naismith,
1861–1939

Below: the YMCA
gym where the
first basketball
games were played

instructors. The two men talked, and Naismith agreed to try to create a new game.

Dr. Gulick gave Dr. Naismith only two general guidelines. First, the new game had to be less rough than soccer, football, rugby, or wrestling. Second, it had to be played indoors. Dr. Gulick wanted a game to fill in the gap between football in the fall and baseball in the spring.

Armed with these guidelines, Dr. Naismith set about his task. He watched other popular games of the time, intending to use some of their good features in his new one, if he could. Naismith knew, of course, that all team games used some kind of ball. Roughness and body contact occurred, he noted, when a person tried to stop the progress of the player with the ball. Thus he would have to find a way to use a ball and yet avoid roughness.

One way to cut down on roughness and body contact was to keep the number of players down. So, for his new game, Naismith decided that seven players would be a good-sized team. Next he set up severe penalties for body contact of any kind. Then he decided that some sort of goal placed above the heads of the players would help even more to cut down on roughness. But what kind of goal?

Suddenly it came to him. Why not have a round goal into which the ball could be *thrown?* This would create an entirely new way of scoring. At the same time, it would wipe out the need for bumping, tackling, and holding.

The next day, with the help of several puzzled students, Naismith tacked an old peach basket to the edge of the balcony in the training school gym. He then got hold of a stray soccer ball and let loose basketball's first shot—an awkward, underhand throw. No one knows any more whether or not it went into the basket. But what we do know is that with that awkward shot, Naismith had given birth to a game that would one day become the most popular spectator sport in the world, one that would be played by more people than any other game in history.

The first official basketball game was played on January 20, 1892. Dr. Naismith nailed a second peach basket to the balcony at the other end of the gym and had the school janitors wait on ladders at each end of the court to retrieve the balls from the baskets. He then explained to a group of people how the game was to be played. Needless to say, this first effort was something less than a great success. The score of this first game is unknown, but we can be fairly sure that the janitors were not overworked that night. The era of the basketball sharpshooter was not yet at hand.

The men on the ladders continued to retrieve balls for many years. Then one day someone thought of cutting the bottom out of the basket so the ball could fall through. Eventually the regular wood peach basket was replaced by a metal basket, which, in turn, was replaced in 1906 by an open loop fixed on a pole or board ten feet (3.05 meters) above the ground.

In many gyms and church halls, however, the basket continued to be tacked to the end balconies, but that arrangement presented a definite problem. Fans, eager to help their team win, would often sit in the balcony seats near the basket. Using their hands, umbrellas, sticks, and even their feet, they would push or steer the ball into or away from the basket, depending on which team they wanted to win. Probably some of basketball's first great scorers were not any of the players on the court at all, but rather, some quick-handed fans who sat in the end balconies.

To end fan participation, backboards were installed behind the baskets. This change had an interesting side effect. The players now had a flat surface against which to bank the ball into the hoop. Some of the sport's best shooters soon developed skill in this.

The first backboards were made of wire mesh, which didn't work too well, since the ball angled off in odd directions when it hit the mesh. Eventually, wooden backboards were substituted. These, in turn, were replaced by the glass backboards used today.

Backboards got in the way of busy balcony fans but did not stop them completely. No longer able to deflect the ball by hand or umbrella, the fans took to shaking the guy wires that held the backboards in place. So in time these wires were placed out of reach of the fans.

In basketball's early years—when the game was played in

**Basketball's early equipment
included a straw peachbasket**

dance halls, parish house basements, converted barns, and tiny school gyms—many courts were completely enclosed by some sort of netting. This may have been done to protect the fans from the players—or vice versa! Another possible reason for the netting may have been to keep the ball in the court. A ball that was tossed by mistake into the crowd was not likely to be seen again. The word *cager,* another name for a basketball player, comes from the fact that these early games were played inside cages of wire or cord netting.

The cord netting presented no particular problems, but as anyone who has ever fallen into chicken wire can guess, playing on a wire-enclosed court was really dangerous. If a court enclosed by chicken wire was being used, the players would wear heavily padded uniforms with long trousers. One club even boasted of having on hand a set of metal-reinforced trunks!

In the early days of basketball, there was almost no outside shooting. Players shot only when they were right under the basket. This led to lots of crowding into a small area of the court. A player who drove for the basket did so at his own risk. More often than not, he wound up sprawled on the floor or plastered against the netting. And if there wasn't any netting he was likely to land two or three rows back in the spectator's seats.

At first basketball had none of the speed or smooth skill of today's game. In fact, the racing-fast basketball game of today would have been impossible under the old rules. The ball was dribbled with two hands, not one, and there was very little movement. Teams had to line up for a jump after each basket, making the fast break impossible. Players worked harder on defensive tactics than on scoring. The referees, such as they were, interpreted Dr. Naismith's original rules very loosely. They would often look the other way while chaos reigned under the basket.

In 1934, however, basketball people got together to agree on one set of rules. Dr. Naismith's brainchild was on its way to becoming the most exciting, crowd-pleasing sport in the world.

**Edward Wachter, one of the
games greatest early centers**

BOWLING

Bowling may have started as part of a primitive religious rite. It has been played in some form or other in various parts of the world for centuries. Stone balls and nine stone pins were found in the tomb of a child buried in Egypt in 5,200 B.C. Paintings on four-thousand-year-old Egyptian vases show royalty playing a game in which a ball was rolled along the ground. The ancient Romans played a game called *boccie,* a term still used for a game played in Italy today.

Historians have evidence, however, that long ago, religious people would often roll stones toward sticks or other objects that represented evil spirits. The goal was to knock over as many of them as possible. It was believed that the more that were knocked, or "bowled" over, the freer the bowler would be from unwanted demons.

This religious superstition may have carried over into Germany. To prove that their souls were pure, the German men would roll a ball along the ground, trying to knock down an object called a *Kegel,* which was shaped like a small Indian club. The men usually played in a church corridor or empty alley, which may account for the narrow width of modern bowling lanes. The term kegling, a synonym for bowling, comes from the German word *Kegel.*

But whatever name or form the game took on during its long history, the object of the game remained the same—to knock over as many pins as possible. In some places a round ball was used; in other places an oblong one was used.

Bowling became popular in England as early as the thirteenth century. People referred to it as "lawn bowling" to distinguish it from other kinds of bowling known at the time. Sir Francis Drake became one of the chief patrons of the game. As legend has it, Sir Francis, in 1588, was bowling against fellow officers when he was told that the Spanish, with whom England was at war, were approaching the English coast. Thus warned, Drake is said to have replied, "There's plenty of time to finish the match and then beat the Spaniards."

The Dutch introduced the game of ninepins to America and made it popular wherever they settled. Perhaps you will recall mention of the sport in the story of Rip Van Winkle. Washington Irving described thunder as like the sound of a ball rolling at pins.

The original ninepins alley was a bed of cinders or clay. As time went on, a board twelve inches (30.48 centimeters) wide replaced the clay. The nine pins were set up in rows of three each.

Before long, however, gambling gave the sport a bad name. Many states banned it. Even where it was not banned, it lost much of its appeal. It is said that the current game of *ten*pins came about as a result of adding another pin to get around local laws that forbade the game of *nine*pins. The bans were eventually lifted, and bowling has become very popular.

A modern bowling alley is quite different from the older versions. Machines now set up the pins and return the balls automatically.

BOXING

Although we can't be sure, boxing probably goes back to prehistoric times, when cavemen argued over such things as who would get the best parts of a slain sabre-toothed tiger. As an organized activity, boxing dates back at least as far as the ancient Roman gladiator contests.

The purpose of the Roman gladiator contests was to hurt and kill. The gladiators wore metal-studded leather wrappings on their hands. Two men would sit on a rock, nose to nose, and take swings at each other until one collapsed. When one fell, the other punched him to death. During it all, the emperor and his people sat by and cheered. Later on, the fighters were told to move around on their feet while they fought. Thus, fighting as we know it today was born. A few centuries later, however, a Roman leader banned the fighting completely when he realized he was losing the services of a lot of men.

Boxing reappeared again in England in the eighteenth century, as brutal as ever. Men fought each other savagely with their bare hands. A round lasted until one fighter fell or was knocked down. The downed fighter had thirty seconds to "get back to scratch," or toe a mark in the turf or on the floor. If he failed to do this, he was declared the loser. Bouts often lasted fifty or sixty rounds. Both fighters were battered, bloodied figures at the end, and it was often difficult to tell who had won.

But about one hundred years ago, the Marquess of Queensberry changed the London Prize Ring rules. He set out to make the sport safer and more appealing. He had the fighters wear padded gloves and limited each round to three minutes, with a minute's rest in between. For the first time, boxing took on an image of respectability.

Boxing has changed dramatically in recent years. It is now usually conducted with a referee and two judges. There is a time-keeper who counts for the knockdowns. In some areas, the referee is the only official. The Marquess of Queensberry rules say there is no butting, heeling, or gouging, and no hitting when a man is down. Any portion of the body below the waist is foul, and when a man is down on one or both knees, he is said to be down.

There are eight weight divisions. They are heavyweight, 175 pounds (79.38 kilograms) and up; light-heavyweight, 161 to 175 pounds (73.03 to 79.38 kilograms); middleweight, 148 to 160 pounds (67.13 to 72.58 kilograms); welterweight, 136 to 147 pounds (61.69 to 66.68 kilograms); lightweight, 127 to 135 pounds (58.26 to 60.85 kilograms); featherweight, 119 to 126 pounds (53.98 to 57.15 kilograms); bantamweight, 113 to 118 pounds (51.26 to 53.53 kilograms); and flyweight, 112 pounds (50.81 kilograms) or less.

The heavyweight class has the richest history in boxing. The others go back barely a hundred years. People didn't seem to want to watch anyone fight except the big fellows. Someone weighing only 125 pounds (56.70 kilograms) or so didn't have a chance at the big money.

The English had a lock on the championship for a couple of centuries. A few outsiders were exceptions to this: John Morrissey, an Irish-American; Paddy Ryan, another Irish-American; and Tom Molineaux, a slave from Virginia.

Two fighters have each held championships in three divisions. Bob Fitzsimmons was middleweight, light-heavyweight, and heavyweight champion. Henry Armstrong held the featherweight, lightweight, and welterweight titles, all within less than a year, and therefore all at the same time!

New York was the first state to make boxing legal. For a while, New York's championship was considered the world title. Today there are two world championships, that of the World Boxing Association and that of the World Boxing Council. Thus it is possible to have two world champions in each weight division at the same time.

Ancient Roman boxing

Sparring in public houses in the 1800s was quite common

In the United States as well as in most other nations, boxing is conducted on three levels: school and college, club, and professional. Those who become successful in the first two categories usually turn professional. College boxing is no longer very popular. Collegians used to fight with headgear, in front of audiences who were permitted to applaud or cheer only between rounds. The pro game boomed in the late 1940s and early 1950s thanks to television. But television stripped the small clubs of their boxers. People stayed away from the clubs to watch the main attractions on TV.

Broadcasts of big fights via closed circuit television came in during the 1960s. Satellite communications opened up far-off places to the major boxing events. Muhammad Ali, heavyweight champion, defended his title in places such as Zaire and the Philippines.

For a long time, the United States supplied the champions for just about every weight division. In recent years, however, foreign talent has taken over from U.S. boxers on a worldwide scale. Recently, the United States has had to settle for the heavyweight crown and perhaps one or two others.

Boxing has provided the means for a fast rise to success for a number of young men from poverty areas. And, interestingly enough, boxing tends to become more popular during difficult economic times, when jobs are hard to get.

FOOTBALL (AMERICAN)

There is no record of the beginning of the game we know in the United States as football. People have probably played with—or at least kicked—some form of ball from the earliest prehistoric times. Preserved in Egyptian tombs are balls thousands of years old, which were once owned by the pharaohs. These balls were made of fine linen or soft leather and were filled with straw or dried grass. Other civilizations made balls by sewing together two round pieces of animal skin and stuffing them with earth, grain, corn husks, or wood chips. Some primitive balls were carved out of light wood. In the 1500s, the Maya Indians, who were living on the Yucatan peninsula, made balls of solid rubber, a material whose usefulness other societies were not to discover until hundreds of years later.

It is generally agreed that football began as part of a religious ceremony in which the ball represented the sun. Large groups would take part in these games. The goal was most often a tree, the symbol of all growing things. Hitting the tree with the ball or whatever object was being kicked was thought to represent the sun with its warmth reaching all growing things. Often these contests lasted for days, until the players fell to the ground exhausted.

Since the ball was supposed to represent the sun, all balls were round in shape. This made them easy to kick but difficult to throw. It was hard to grip the round surface with the fingers and the palm of the hand. This may well be why primitive football consisted of kicking and not throwing.

Much of the early history of football is the history of soccer as well. The game Europeans refer to as football is what is called soccer in the United States today. U.S. football is derived from soccer through the British game of rugby. It is often hard to sort out which elements come from which.

Football was very popular in the ancient world. Some versions of the game were played in ancient Greece and Rome. There is evidence in classical literature that the football played by the early Greeks was more refined than the primitive kicking contests mentioned earlier. For example, there was one game in which the players tried to carry a ball across a line defended by the other side.

It is believed that the Romans copied the Greek version of football and enjoyed it for many years. Then one day Caesar Augustus banned the game because it was "too gentle for war preparation." Later, after the ban was lifted, the Romans played a game called *harpastum,* meaning "I seize." From this we can guess that in this game, too, the ball was probably carried.

To the Romans, football was more than a pastime. It was used to prepare for warfare and conquests. It may have been Roman soldiers who first introduced the game to Britain. There are even reports that people of Derby, England, played a game of football to celebrate a victory over these very same Romans in A.D. 217.

Some historians claim it was the Normans, not the Romans, who brought football to Britain. They support this theory by pointing out that references to the game occur in English literature only after the Norman conquest of 1066.

The English hated the Normans. One story, very likely more imaginative than factual, may have developed out of this hatred.

Many years after the Norman invasion, English workmen, digging on the site of an old battlefield, unearthed the skull of a fallen Norman soldier. They began kicking the grisly souvenir back and forth across the field. Other skulls found at the site suffered the same indignities. After a short time, it was almost like a game. What a kick in the head the dead Normans got! The workmen eventually split into equal sides and tried to kick the skulls past each other. When the supply of skulls ran short, they used the bladders of goats or sheep stuffed with grass. These balls were easier on the toes anyway.

The first description of football appeared in London in 1175. William Fitzstephen wrote that "the youth of the city went outside the city for the famous game of ball." It wasn't until 1486, however, that the word football was used to describe the game.

In its early years, football was called by several names, including bigside, wall game, and kick ball. By any name, however, the game was a wild mob scene. There were no limits on the number of players. Sometimes two or three hundred men would be on a side. They would square off against a force of equal size in an open area, usually well outside town, because the local officials feared for the safety of the rest of the townspeople. The purpose of the game was to see which of the two groups could kick the ball to the opponents' end of the field the most number of times. Sometimes there were contests between whole towns. Opposing teams would meet halfway between the towns and drop the ball. The idea was to kick the ball to the other side's town square or village green. Often these wild battles raged for hours as the players kicked the ball—and each other—across fields, down dirt roads, through cattle pens, and over hills.

The first college football game played in the United States was actually a soccer match. It took place on November 6, 1869, in New Jersey. Rutgers played Princeton. There were twenty-five players on each side and two hundred spectators. Rutgers won, six goals to four. Two other "firsts" may have happened during this historic first game. Many Rutgers players, to show off their team, wore scarlet jerseys or caps. These were the first football uniforms. Princeton students led their team on with the first football cheer. The students may have gotten it from a Civil War army yell used when Union soldiers marched through Princeton in 1861.

Except for the scarlet jerseys or caps worn in that first game, early football players wore no special uniforms. But in 1877 the Princeton players showed up for a game with Harvard in orange and black striped jerseys. Harvard was very upset by the uniforms but won anyway, and soon other colleges began using uniforms.

In time, changes in the uniforms were made for safety's sake. Helmets first appeared around 1900. They were made of soft leather, not, of course, the hard plastic of today. Before that, players had worn wool caps. If they didn't wear caps, they would let their

Above: an early football game at Rugby College.
Right: Pudge Heffelfinger was the first known football
pro. He received $500 for playing a game in 1892.

hair grow long and knot it across the top of the head to form a cushion. As for the football itself, when the forward pass became legal in the early 1900s, its shape was streamlined to allow for a better grip.

For more details about the history of American football, see the chapter on soccer.

GOLF

The first shot in the game we call golf may have been made by a lonely Scottish shepherd many centuries ago. According to legend, a shepherd, bored by his work, passed the time by hitting small round stones along the ground with his staff. By chance one of his shots rolled into a nearby rabbit hole. At the time, the shepherd didn't think much of his "hole in one." Then a friend challenged him to repeat it. He tried, but with little success. His friend then started hitting stones toward the rabbit hole. He didn't do much better. History's opening golf match would hardly have made a modern-day pro envious.

Many people credit Scotland with being the birthplace of golf as we know it today. However, the game is probably an adaptation of similar games that have been played throughout history in different parts of the world. The Romans had a game known as *paganica,* which was something like golf. The Dutch game of *kolven* is a distant relative of present-day golf. The Dutch point out that many of the words used in modern golf are derived from Dutch words. A *kolf,* for instance, was a club, and a *tuitje* was a small mound of earth on which to place the ball before hitting it (pronounced properly in Dutch, *tuitje* sounds a lot like the word "tee"). The Dutch also use the expression *Stuit mij,* meaning roughly "It stops me." This could be where we got the modern word "stymie," which is used when a player's path to the green is blocked by a tree or other obstacle. And there are some who say that the modern word *putt* comes from the Dutch *putten,* meaning "to place in a hole."

[37]

But wherever golf got its start, Scotland is the place where the game was first recorded and grew famous. In fact, golf grew so popular in Scotland that in 1457 Parliament banned it—people were so busy playing golf that they didn't do the things they were supposed to do. The ban didn't last too long, however.

Scotland's famed St. Andrews golf course was built in 1754. The world's first golf tournament was held at Prestwick, Scotland, in 1860. Golf's first playing rules were set down at St. Andrews in 1882.

The first object hit by a golf stick was probably a round stone or a rounded piece of wood. The first official ball was a small bag of thin leather, stuffed firm with feathers. In 1848, the gutta-percha ball was invented. Gutta-percha is a rubbery substance gotten from certain trees in Malaya. This ball proved superior because it could be hit farther and with more accuracy. Rubber-core balls came into use in 1899 and have been used, with certain improvements, ever since.

The original clubs were nothing more than tree branches bent or curved at one end. Then came separate wooden heads attached to sticks. These were followed by iron clubheads on hickory or bamboo shafts. We now use steel, aluminum, or graphite shafts and iron clubheads.

No one used golf bags at first. The clubs were simply carried loose. Then one day in 1870, a retired sailmaker used a piece of leftover canvas to keep his clubs dry in the rain. This led to the use of flimsy canvas golf bags, which were later replaced by the heavier leather ones.

Before the first golf course was built, at Leith, Scotland, in 1744, local golfers played the game over stretches of empty land near the Irish Sea. Present-day Scottish and Irish courses still keep many of the features of these wild, wind-lashed seaside "courses."

Golf did not always have eighteen holes. Some early layouts numbered five or six; others had fourteen. On the fourteen-hole courses, golfers would play the fourteen holes on the way out and then play them again on the way back in. This meant they actually played twenty-eight holes. St. Andrews at first had nine holes. It

**The game of golf,
early 1900s**

later added a parallel nine holes, and the eighteen there became the standard.

We know that golf was played in the United States at the time of the American Revolution. Scottish officers in the British army played while they were serving in the American colonies. The Scots spread their love of golf to all parts of the British Empire—Canada, Australia, India, and various other Asian outposts.

Golf played by North Americans, however, is less than a century old. Credit for its introduction goes to John G. Reid, a Scot who settled in Yonkers, New York. In February of 1888, Reid laid out a six-hole course on a lot near his home. Four neighbors joined him, creating what was to become the fabled Apple Tree Gang. They were called this because they met under a giant apple tree and left their coats and picnic lunches there during the matches. Before long, they picked up many other enthusiasts. They decided they needed a clubhouse. St. Andrews Golf Club, named for the famed Scottish course, became the first American club for golfers.

Up to the early part of the twentieth century, the greatest golfers came from Great Britain. Then Bobby Jones, a U.S. citizen, took the U.S. Amateur, U.S. Open, British Amateur, and British Open titles all in the same year, 1928. Jones's "grand slam" began the rise of the golf game in the United States. American women as well as American men are some of the world's outstanding golfers, and play for large amounts of prize money. Some ten million people play the game today in the United States. The golf industry—making and selling equipment, clothing, courses—is a huge business.

GYMNASTICS

China, Persia (now Iran), and India all claim to have been the first to start gymnastics. But all we know for sure is that gymnastics can definitely be traced as far back as ancient Greece. The Greeks gave the sport its name. *Gymnos* is a Greek word meaning naked, which is how the Greeks worked out. From *gymnos* came the word gymnasium, which meant "a school for naked exercise."

At first, the Greek gymnasiums were used only to train athletes for the Olympics. Later, however, they became social gathering places, centers of community affairs. Every Greek city had at least one; Athens even had three.

The Romans borrowed the sport from the Greeks and then added to it. They introduced the wooden horse, on which their soldiers exercised and worked on military moves. This same piece of equipment, with minor changes, is still used in competition today.

Modern international gymnastics competition is made up of six events for men and four for women. The men's events include floor exercises, horizontal bar, long horse (or vaulting horse), parallel bars, rings (or still rings as they are sometimes called), and the side horse. The women's events include vaulting horse, uneven parallel bars, floor exercises, and the balance beam.

The forms of gymnastics as we know them today were developed to a high degree of specialization by the Germans in the 1880s. The Germans and other European countries dominated gymnastic competition in the Olympics from 1896 until 1960, when Japan managed to break through that continuous winning record.

**Gymnastics
in ancient Greece**

In recent years, gymnastics has begun to be taken more and more seriously in the United States, partly because of the greater number of, and improvements in, the gymnastic programs in high schools and colleges, especially those for girls and women.

The rest of the world, however, isn't waiting for the United States to catch up. The Russians are getting better all the time. They have amazing performers such as Olga Korbut and Ludmilla Turischeva. The Eastern Europeans, including the sensational teen-age Rumanian Olympic star Nadia Comaneci, and the Japanese are also at work perfecting moves on the bars, rings, and horses, and becoming more daring than ever before.

Gymnastics, one of the most ancient of all athletic pastimes, may well be the international sport of the future.

A Horse that you can keep in your House.

VIGOR'S
RSE-ACTION SADDLE.

Personally ordered by
H.R.H. THE PRINCESS OF WALES.

rfect Substitute for Horse-Riding.

A Healthy, Stimulating Exercise.

HEALTH WITHOUT DRUGS.

ILN OCT 5 1895

use of Vigor's Horse-Action Saddle is a sure cure of

INDIGESTION, NERVOUSNESS,
SSITUDE,   LIVER COMPLAINT,
SLOW CIRCULATION.

culars, Illustrations, and Testimonials, Post Free.

Vigor; 21, Baker St London.

Some typical advertisements
selling health through
gymnastics in the 1800s

HOCKEY

Field and ice hockey are slightly different games. Field hockey is played on land rather than on ice and uses a ball instead of a hard rubber puck. Ice hockey dates back only about a century or so. Some form of field hockey, on the other hand, may have been played as far back as four thousand years ago in Persia.

In 478 B.C., the Greeks built a sea wall near Athens. Remnants of it were discovered by workmen in 1922. At the base of this wall, there is a scene carved in the stone of two athletes holding sticks that look a lot like hockey sticks. The sticks are crossed over a ball, and the pose is not unlike the face-off that opens modern-day ice hockey games. This proves that hockey dates back at least twenty-five centuries.

Historians think the Greeks introduced field hockey to the Romans and Roman legions spread the game to other parts of the world. In Britain, hockey took various forms, including games called Scottish shinty, English bandy, and Irish hurling. In all these games, a ball was hit across the turf with a crooked stick.

Irish hurling, a ferocious game, may have been the closest thing to modern field hockey. It was played in Ireland long before the time of St. Patrick and traveled across to England, where it became the less violent bandy ball. The name hockey can be traced to the old French word *hoquet,* meaning shepherd's crook, or stick.

The history of field hockey in England is easy to trace. In 1174, there were references in writings to "the stick and ball game." This could have been bandy ball. In 1333, images of hockey players were engraved on altar decorations. The stained-glass windows of Gloucester Cathedral, built in 1360, show a hockey game of sorts. In 1365, King Edward III outlawed bandy ball; it was interfering with his subjects' daily archery practice.

The hockey games of this era were violent and undisciplined. Rival players struck each other unmercifully with their sticks. Injuries were common and deaths were not unheard of. A player who tried to prevent the winning goal was truly in danger. Eventually, though, rules were set down to reduce the violence. One rule forbade raising the stick above shoulder level. This rule is the cornerstone of hockey safety to this day.

Probably no form of ice hockey dates back earlier than A.D. 1000. At this time, European youths first tied sharpened bones to their boots using leather thongs, and began skating on frozen ponds. For fun, they probably soon took to batting a ball or a small stone across the ice with sticks, tree limbs, or poles.

Holland claims credit for first combining field hockey and ice skating to create ice hockey. The first such games, the Dutch say, took place in their country around 1700. English, Scottish, and Irish historians, however, claim that *their* ancestors were *also* playing ice hockey—or some crude form of it—around the same time.

There are even conflicting versions of how the game got started in Canada. Some think the first game of ice hockey ever played in Canada took place in February 1837, in Montreal, between the Dorchester Club and the Uptown Club. After Dorchester scored the first goal, the crowd jumped onto the ice and a great fight began. When the fans refused to leave the ice, Dorchester claimed victory. Even then, hockey stirred fierce passions among its fans.

Conflicting historical evidence says that Kingston, Ontario, was the site of the first Canadian ice hockey contest. The year was 1855, and the players were English soldiers serving with the Royal Canadian Rifles at Kingston. As the story goes, the soldiers found some old ice skates, swept snow off the iced up water behind their barracks, and played ice hockey. This could have happened. Kingston had been the site of the annual Canadian shinty matches for many

Found at the base of an ancient Greek statue, this frieze seems to show the start of a hockey game.

Hockey being played on the skating rink at McGill University, Montreal, around 1865.

years. The people of that area knew the rules. All they had to do was adapt the game to ice.

Still another claim exists for what was the first ice hockey game. This one is made for McGill University in Montreal. G. F. Robertson, a McGill student, saw a game of field hockey on a trip to England. He was a fine ice skater and saw the possibilities for playing the game on ice. When he came back to Canada, Robertson and fellow McGill students devised a game combining the basic idea of field hockey with the speed of ice skating. It soon became the craze at McGill. By 1880, the McGill University Ice Hockey Club was formed.

Hockey in those days was played by a seven-member team. A pair of portable poles, often with no net between them, was the goal. Goal judges, who stood right behind the poles, wore no protective padding. For the most part, players provided their own equipment. Sticks of all different lengths and shapes were used in the same game. And the games, all played outdoors, were at the mercy of the Canadian winter weather.

It wasn't until a uniform code of rules was established that ice hockey really came into its own. McGill University, called the cradle of ice hockey, deserves most of the credit for solving the sport's early problems. The McGill rules called for six players on a side. A net or cage replaced the two poles as a goal. A puck, or flat disk, replaced the rubber ball. When the McGill players decided to use a flat disk, they had to create one. One bright undergraduate sliced a section one inch thick out of the middle of a hard rubber ball, thus creating the first official hockey puck. Its size and shape are almost the same to this day.

Ice hockey from the 1880s on became very popular in many Canadian cities. One of hockey's most enthusiastic fans was Lord Stanley of Preston, then governor-general of Canada. To encourage further growth of the game, he invested ten pounds sterling (about $48 at the time) in a silver bowl. Beginning in 1893, this bowl was to be awarded annually to the best hockey team in Canada. The governor-general wanted to be forever associated with ice hockey, so he gave the new prize his own name—the Stanley Cup. The Stanley Cup is still awarded annually to the championship team, and is prized as the symbol of hockey's best.

ICE SKATING

Skating on ice was used as a means of travel before it became a sport. Long ago, in the frigid northern countries, people tied crude bone runners to the soles of their shoes, using rawhide thongs. This way they could more easily get across the frozen rivers, ponds, and streams that stood between them and wherever they wanted to go. Later on, the runners were made from wood. By the sixteenth century, crude iron runners appeared. Today, steel blades that are carefully sharpened and finely balanced are used.

The word *skate* seems to have come from the Dutch word *schaats* (pronounced as *sk,* not *sh*). But we are not sure who—the Dutch, Finns, Swedes, or Norwegians—were the first to use skates on frozen waters.

People soon saw that skating could be a sport. Some wanted to show off fancy moves. Others enjoyed racing. From these early activities come our modern ice skating sports of figure skating and speed skating.

The first recognized routines for figure skaters were devised by Jackson Haines, an American ballet master. Moving around Europe, where skating was the craze in the mid-nineteenth century, he taught his routines to young skaters. At the time it was called fancy skating.

Although fancy skating attracted a small group of fans, the general public didn't care much about it. Then Sonja Henie came along in the late 1920s and changed all that. This Norwegian-born skating star won three Olympic skating titles and made a dozen Holly-

Ice skating in the 1700s.
Note the curlicued toes on the skates.

wood movies. She introduced her art to millions of boys and girls. Since then, many of the world's champion figure skaters have been from the United States, among them Tenley Albright, Dick Button, Peggy Fleming, Janet Lynn, and Dorothy Hamill.

The United States, however, has not produced many strong speed skaters. Most of the world's champion speed skaters have been Euorpean. Speed events are held at distances of 500, 1,500, 5,000, and 10,000 meters.

Skate sailing is a fairly modern addition to the sport of ice skating. It was first popular in the northeastern United States. It is just what its name says it is—a sail, used to catch the wind, that helps the skater move across the ice. With the cooperation of the wind, the skater can reach speeds greater than could ever be achieved under leg power alone. Skate sailing is a dangerous but exciting sport.

Ice skating in Central Park,
New York City, 1894

LACROSSE

Lacrosse is truly a game of many cultures. It was invented by North American Indians, was named by French missionaries, and has become the national game of Canada.

Canadian Plains Indians called their game *baggataway.* There were anywhere from fifty to two hundred players to a side. The object of the game was to get the ball into an area occupied by local medicine men. The playing field boundaries were not strictly laid out, and the playing rules were followed loosely, if at all. Games lasted for many hours, and ended only when players fell down from exhaustion or had been clubbed to their knees by rough opponents.

Baggataway matches included pre-game feasts, post-game dances, and a highly festive atmosphere throughout. The women were the loudest and most enthusiastic fans. If they thought a player was losing interest in the game, they would sometimes beat him with whippy tree branches as he trotted near the sideline.

French missionaries who watched these games thought the sticks used by the Indians looked like crosiers—bishops' staffs, which look like shepherds' crooks. So they called the game *la crosse,* and took news of it back to Canadian cities. After a while, the name of the game became, simply, lacrosse.

The first formal games were played in Montreal in 1834, but the rules in use today didn't come into being until thirty-three years later. In 1867, Dr. George Beers, a Montreal dentist, drew up a set of regulations for the game. Twelve players were given regular positions. (The team was reduced to ten players in 1933.) A hard

**North American Indians
playing the game of lacrosse**

rubber ball replaced the leather one stuffed with hair the Indians had used. That same year, the Canadian Parliament adopted lacrosse as the national game.

It was in New England that lacrosse first appeared in the United States. There are records of its being played at Gilmore's Gardens in New York City in 1877. New York University, Princeton, and Harvard served as leaders in introducing it as a college sport. From the East, lacrosse spread throughout the nation.

The most important international competition was held in 1930. It was between the college all-stars from the United States and Oxford-Cambridge. In 1932, a crowd of some one hundred and fifty thousand watched lacrosse being played in the Olympics. This was the largest lacrosse crowd ever.

On the club level, Baltimore leads as the city most involved in lacrosse. Crowds of ten thousand are not unusual there for big games between the Mt. Washington Club and college teams such as Navy, Johns Hopkins, or the University of Maryland.

A touring team of Canadian Indians played a game of lacrosse before Queen Victoria in the 1860s. By 1877, the British were playing lacrosse regularly. In the early 1900s, it was modified somewhat for women and played in private schools. The sport is now played in a number of girls' schools in Britain, although the version the girls play is not as rough as that handed down from the Indians. The emphasis of the game today is on skill and speed. Because body contact is not allowed, protective equipment is not needed.

Introduction of professional lacrosse was tried several times, both in Canada and in the United States. The effort was not very successful in either place. One problem was the game was played in the summer, and people didn't want to sit indoors in a hot arena. Air conditioning has helped, however, and another well-financed attempt, somewhat more successful, was made to get a lacrosse league going in the United States in the mid-1970s.

SKIING

We can't be sure just *where* skiing began. However, there is no doubt about *how* it began. In northern Europe and Asia, deep snow blanketed the land most of the year. Ancient peoples moving from place to place are known to have experimented with crude footwear for easier going in the snow. Those primitive efforts probably resulted in history's first snowshoe. This was a help, but not the answer.

We can guess that one day someone walking down a steep icy hill started to slide. Amazingly, the trip to the bottom was accomplished in record time. And it was much easier than legging it one step at a time through the snow.

History's first skier was probably quite pleased with the discovery and set about to improve his or her sliding shoes. Smooth wooden slats attached to the shoes were the result. We know this because the word *ski* comes from a northern European word meaning "a splinter cut from a log."

How old is skiing? Well, a pair of skis in a Swedish museum is thought to be at least five thousand years old. Stone carvings in a Norwegian cave, said to date back at least four thousand years, show skiing. And by the seventh century A.D. the Chinese were writing about it.

Skis helped people travel and hunt in the frigid Scandinavian countries for centuries before anyone thought about using them for sport. Then, in the eighteenth century, Norwegian soldiers on skis took part in a sporting contest in what is now the city of Oslo. Zig-

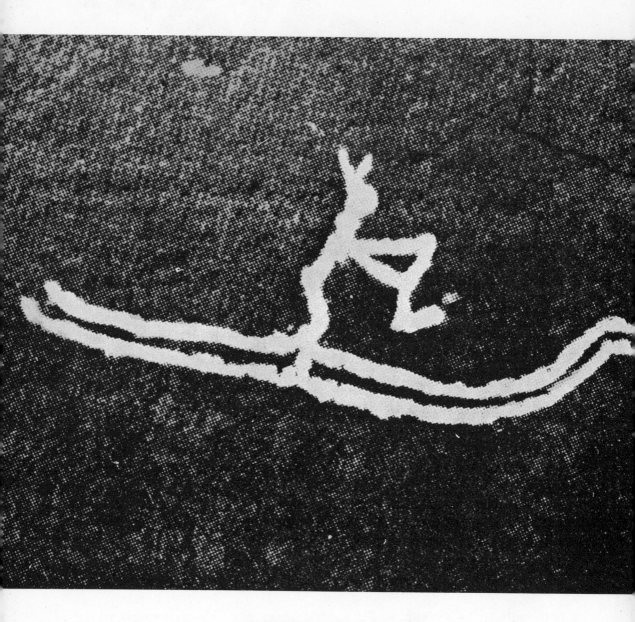

**Above: a carving on a rock
belonging to the Stone Age,
found in northern Norway**

**Right: Lapp skier-hunters,
as illustrated in a book
published in 1682**

zagging between bushes and trees on their way down the slope, they accidentally hit on the idea of the slalom. The slalom today is one of skiing's most popular and demanding events.

In the 1850s, the Norwegians began holding annual competitions in the valley of Telemark. They developed a means of holding the heel in place on the ski, thereby making the first ski jump possible, which took place on Norway's Huseby Hill, in 1879. In 1883, two main kinds of skiing—cross-country racing and jumping—were separated out for competition purposes.

During the next few decades, the new and exciting sport from Norway spread to almost every country that had snow, including England. It was in England that standards and rules for the modern slalom were officially set down, even though slalom is a Scandinavian word (*sla* means "slope" and *lom* means "track left in the snow").

Skiing has grown extremely popular in the United States. The first U.S. ski club was organized in 1867 in, believe it or not, Laporte, California!

Today, wherever you can find a mountain and some snow, you are likely to see cars with ski racks on their roofs heading for the slopes and bumpers on the cars displaying stickers saying, "Think snow!"

SOCCER (RUGBY FOOTBALL)

Games much like soccer have been played for centuries all over the world. In fact, a game of a similar nature may have been played in the ancient world. But it was in England that the modern version of the sport got its start. The English gave soccer its name and drew up the first playing rules, which subsequently led to two American sports many centuries later.

The English may have been playing at least some form of soccer as early as A.D. 217. But in 1175, William Fitzstephen of London wrote that "the youth of the city went outside the city for the famous game of ball." This is the first written mention of the game.

So many young people began playing it that, in 1314, King Edward II banned the game. He threatened to imprison anyone caught playing it. Such games got in the way of other activities, such as preparing for battle. But finally, in 1603, King James I lifted the ban and even urged his subjects to play it. He thought it was good for them.

From that point on, the game rapidly grew in popularity. Teams from rival towns engaged each other in wild matches called "futballe." In Ireland, the rough-and-tumble sport of Gaelic football became almost a national pastime.

In these matches, each town or district had its own style of play and its own rules. Players from rural areas may have favored a wide-open style. London players, on the other hand, learned the game on narrow cobblestone streets. Thus, they probably became good at dribbling and passing the ball with their feet. When these

[59]

two groups came together, they each brought their own element—and helped form the exciting game we have today.

Remember, when we talk of the European game of football, we refer to the game in the United States known as soccer. The chapter in this book on football tells how the popular U.S. game evolved from this original "football."

The first unified soccer rules were drawn up at Cambridge University in 1848. They were refined again in 1862. By that time, soccer clubs were springing up throughout Britain and wherever the British people went as missionaries, teachers, seamen, or traders. In 1863, most clubs joined the Football Association. In fact, one theory of how soccer got its name is that the students used the letters *s, o,* and *c* from *Association* as a base for a slang term for the game. Another theory claims that the name refers to the knee-high socks worn by most players at the time. We do not know which theory is correct.

We do know, however, that North American football is related to soccer—but not directly. The direct relation is to the game of rugby.

The rules of soccer were rather loosely defined during the early 1800s, but there was one rule common to all variations of the game: the ball could never be touched by the hands or carried. It could be moved only by the feet. This is the way everyone played the game. Then things changed. One theory of how and when the rules changed comes to us from Warwickshire, England. Unfortunately, there is little evidence to back up this theory. But it is fun to tell anyway.

One afternoon in 1823 at the Rugby School in Warwickshire, a student named William Webb Ellis was taking part in an interclass soccer match, or bigside, as it was called. The game was supposed to end at 5:00 P.M. It was getting close to that time, and there was no score on either side. With an eye on the big tower clock and bored by the slowness of the action, Ellis suddenly scooped up the loose ball in his hands and ran toward the goal. His opponents, startled and angered by such a disregard for the rules, gave chase. But Ellis made it across the goal, with the ball tucked firmly under his arm.

Rugby football, early 1900s

Word of Ellis's run spread to other schools and other teams. Some players began to wonder if running with the ball was such a bad idea after all.

Whether this story is true or not, the game did change around this time. It wasn't until 1839, however, that the new game got its name. Arthur Pell, a student at Cambridge, suggested to friends that they "have a go at the game at Rugby." The name stuck, and rugby football was on its way. At first, running with the ball was permitted only after fair catches. In time, however, the rules were changed and running with the ball was allowed all the time.

In Ellis's day, any number of players could take part in the rugby game. Eventually, the size of the team was reduced to twenty, then fifteen, and then eleven. It is now fifteen again.

Rugby arrived in the United States by way of Canada. In 1874, Harvard University invited a team from McGill University in Montreal to play a "football" game. As the teams warmed up, Harvard players were surprised to see their Canadian visitors running with the ball and passing it with their hands. Handling the ball was against the U.S. game rules!

But the Harvard players were good hosts. They decided to play the first half under the U.S. rules and the second half under McGill's rules. The game ended in a scoreless tie. But the Harvard players liked this new kind of football. It allowed for interesting strategy and clever individual play.

In 1876, Harvard talked Yale into playing a game under rugby rules. Intercollegiate football was changing. Soon it looked very little like English soccer or even rugby. It was truly coming into its own. The new game was fast, wide open, and daring—at least by the standards of the day.

Thus, what is often considered as the first college "football" game played in the United States, a match between Rutgers and Princeton in 1869, was really a soccer match.

Today we can see the two paths the game of soccer has taken. In North American football, the ball is both kicked and carried. Players tackle each other to prevent advances with the ball. U.S. soccer is almost the same as the game called football in Europe. The ball is mostly kicked, not carried. Fancy footwork is the key to success.

SOFTBALL

Softball can be traced back to the 1880s' version of baseball. Several groups, working separately from one another, were trying to bring baseball indoors. To do this, they first made the ball larger and softer to slow down the action. Then they made the bat shorter and lighter and shortened the distance between home plate and the pitcher's mound. Finally they put the four bases closer together. When they were done, they had a game that could be played in gymnasiums and field houses—even in barns—while the winter winds howled outside and the snow piled high on regular baseball diamonds. And when spring arrived, the game could simply be moved outside. It became popular instantly.

The game once known as indoor baseball, kitten ball, and mush ball has gained international popularity in the last two decades. Rules are firmly established by an international governing body. Softball has become quite popular in Canada, South America, Australia, and countries in the Far East, as well as in the United States, where it originated.

The reasons for softball's appeal are the same today as they were back in the 1880s. The game can be played on a smaller field than baseball and requires only a minimum of equipment. Only the catcher and first baseman really need gloves. The ball rarely gets lost. More people, even those who are not such good athletes, can play.

At first softball was designed for ten players. There were the nine positions of regular baseball, plus a short fielder. The short fielder was stationed somewhere between the infield and the out-field, depending on how well the batter could hit. Recently, however, the tenth player has been eliminated. This had the effect of opening up the game and giving the offensive side more of a chance to score.

Slow-pitch softball is exactly what the name says. The pitcher delivers the ball with a slow underhand motion. This gives the batter every possible chance to slam it far outfield or at least whack it over second base.

The fast-pitch game of softball is quite different. This is the "big league" version of the sport. Pitchers fire the ball toward the plate with almost as much speed as a regular baseball pitcher. These pitchers can throw curves, drops, hooks—any number of pitches. The pitch they depend on most is the fast ball. It is often in the catcher's mitt before the batter even knows it's been thrown. No-hit no-run games are common in fast-pitch softball.

Fast-pitch softball requires great skill and is very exciting to watch. The slow-pitch game, however, is really the most popular in the U.S. Anyone with the urge to hit a ball and run the bases can take it up. And a great many do.

SQUASH

The game of squash, or squash racquets, as we know it today, may well have started in jail. It is said that inmates of London's Fleet Prison were bored and dreamed up a game to keep themselves busy. Of course they had a lot of time and little space. So they passed the hours by banging a ball against the walls with a wooden paddle. Soon they were playing angle shots off the walls of the narrow halls and box-like cells. This game of racquets, as it was then called, soon spread to other prisons throughout Britain. But its popularity grew very slowly on the outside, most likely because the British thought of it as a game criminals played.

Around 1850, however, racquets was introduced into the British public school system, the first racquets court being built at the Harrow School in Middlesex, just outside of London. Soon the game became so popular that there was usually a long wait to get onto the courts. Some say the new game of squash racquets came about when some players at the Harrow School, who did not like waiting for the courts, decided to make up a game they could play in a smaller space, indoors or out. Another theory that has been put forth to explain the evolution of the game is that squash was the warm-up game the Harrow students played as they waited for their turn on the regular racquets court.

Because the new game was played on a smaller court or in a smaller room, it made sense to use a slower ball. So the Harrow lads used a soft rubber ball. It was so soft, in fact, that you could

squash it with your hand. It also made a squishing sound when it hit the wall. For these reasons, squash racquets soon became the name of the game.

From the Harrow School the game spread to other public schools, to universities and colleges, and to local clubs. All kinds of people, from the poor right up to the king of England, played the new game. It was fast. It was fun. And it could be played in a small space, indoors or out.

British army officers spread the game throughout the world. For a while, its popularity in the United States was confined mostly to the wealthy, in prep schools and colleges. Recently, however, many more young people seem to be taking to the game.

Above: Fleet Prison, London
where the game of squash was born

Below: the game of racquets, 1788

SWIMMING

The world's first swimmer was most likely an innovative caveperson who decided it might be easier and faster to paddle across a river, like the animals, than to build a bridge of logs and walk across. Thus, what we call the dog paddle was probably the first swimming stroke ever used by human beings to propel themselves through deep water.

Swimming, like running, quickly became a necessity for primitive people. They were always on the move, always fleeing from predatory animals. Streams, rivers, ponds, and lakes were all barriers to be crossed. Since boats weren't used until much later, the caveperson had no choice but to swim. Style was not important. Neither was time. Unless, of course, a hungry crocodile was close behind.

Although we can guess some things about how people swam in ancient times, the oldest actual record we have is a scene on a mosaic dug up in Pompeii of men propelling themselves in water. Even before Roman times, however, the ancient Greeks may have taken part in swimming on a grand scale. The country itself has many rivers and beaches, and the Greeks were interested in all kinds of athletics. Being a highly competitive people, they may have been the first to stage swimming contests.

As a sport, swimming did not become really popular in Britain until around 1875, when Captain Matthew Webb, using the breaststroke, successfully swam across the English Channel. Captain Webb's feat proved, once and for all, that human beings could be at home in the water, and that tides and ocean waves could be overcome. All that remained now was to develop new methods of swimming and to gain speed in the water.

The history of the 100-yard event shows the general direction of developments in swimming over the years. Until 1900, the British were more successful in this event than the people of any other country. Then the U.S. swimmers began to lower the time greatly. The development of the freestyle stroke was closely tied to the faster speed. The dog paddle may have been sure, but it wasn't fast. The first attack on the 100-yard distance was with the breaststroke in 1878. The time recorded was 76.75 seconds. A second attempt that same year was clocked at 68.5 seconds.

Changes had begun to appear in the style of British swimming even before these events, however. An Englishman named Trudgen, while on a trip to South America in the 1860s, observed the people there doing a swimming stroke in which the arms came out of the water, one following the other in windmill style. He also observed how fast the swimmers were moving forward in the water. Trudgen brought the stroke back to England and taught it to swimmers there. In addition to the arm motion, the stroke involved a scissor-like kicking movement of the legs. In time, by using this improved stroke, British competitors managed to lower the 100-yard mark to a flat 60 seconds. But that was only the beginning.

The crawl stroke, forerunner of today's freestyle, came on the scene in 1902. That year, Richard Cavill set a world record of 58.6 seconds for 100 yards. He used a new method—the crawl. This story actually began in the late 1880s, when Richard's father (who in 1877 had tried to swim the English Channel and failed) traveled with his family to the South seas. During his trip he noticed the same stroke Trudgen had seen in South America. But Cavill was more concerned with the leg movements. The Cavill family eventually settled in Australia. There they introduced this new and faster method of swimming, different from the others because of its greater attention to leg motions. One of Cavill's sons described the stroke as "a way of crawling through the water," so it became known as the Australian crawl. The new stroke became famous the world over.

The crawl created a new generation of swift swimmers. Duke Kahanamoku, a strong-armed Hawaiian, went the 100 yards in 54.6

Above: an 1872 attempt to swim the English Channel

Right: ladies' swimming fashions and fads in the 1880s.

seconds in 1913. Four years later he lowered his time to 53 seconds, a record that stood for nine years. Then Johnny Weissmuller came along in 1922 with a 52.6 clocking. Today, swimming records are broken almost as fast as they are set.

The crawl, or freestyle, is the only major stroke whose origin can be fairly easily traced. The breaststroke is a close relative of the simple dog paddle and was probably used, on and off, by swimmers before the development of the freestyle. The butterfly is a modern stroke. It probably evolved over a long period of time through the efforts of many different swimmers and swimming coaches. Likewise, the exact origin of the backstroke is difficult to trace. In all probability, it evolved as swimmers, becoming more expert at the standard strokes available to them, experimented with other methods of moving through the water. We can be sure, however, that all competitive swimming was originally based on the crawl stroke.

TENNIS

Historians can't quite agree on where and when tennis began. In thirteenth-century France, there was a game called *la paume,* or the palm game, so called because a ball was propelled across a net by hitting it with the palm of the hand. Later on, wooden rackets or paddles were used, which supplied more force to the various strokes and saved the palm from blistering.

La paume was originally an outdoor game. Early in its history, however, French clergymen began to play it indoors. We suspect they did this because they thought it undignified for priests to be on public display while playing. King Louis IX of France thought it undignified for the clergy to be playing it at all, so he prohibited them from doing so. Louis could not, however, keep the game from becoming popular throughout France.

Tennis may have acquired its name from a command often heard on the courts during games of la paume: *Tenez!* The command when translated means "Take it! Play!" From hearing that word called out, the English-speaking spectators deduced that the name of the game was tennez. In time, the name became tennis. Another possibility is that the name comes from the French word *tamis,* meaning "sieve." In la paume, the ball was bounced on a sieve.

In any event, English observers took the new game back to Britain. There it became quickly popular. Sometime during the four-teenth century, England's Edward III got excited about it and had a court installed in the palace. This was the second time the

**Above left: the game of la paume,
played in France in the 1500s.**

Below left: a tennis court of the 1600s

**Above: lawn tennis at Prospect Park,
New York, 1886**

game went indoors. Edward played the game with much enthusiasm. Thousands of his subjects did the same, and tennis hit a new high in popularity.

We don't know a great deal about the tennis played then. We know that a net has been used throughout most of the game's history. It is also possible that at some early time a wall was used in part of the play. But there seems to have been no regulation size for the court or standards for the type of ball or racket used.

There are believed to have been more than two thousand tennis courts in France during the seventeenth century. A keen tennis rivalry developed between the English and the French. But the tennis enthusiasts, it seemed, weren't so much interested in national pride as they were in money. Betting on tennis matches became big business. It got so bad that France imposed a national ban on the game. Soon after, England did the same. Tennis could have disappeared from the sports scene entirely. The nobility, however, continued to play on indoor private courts and thereby kept the game alive.

Tourists from the United States heard about tennis in the early nineteenth century and brought it home with them. Before long the interest had spread all over the country. The name of the game played at the time was court tennis. It was played in clubs and at private homes.

Lawn tennis as we know it today was started by Major Walter Wingfield at an outdoor party he gave in Wales in 1873. He patented his version of the game under the name of Sphairistike. (It is not really known why he chose this name, but in a short time it disappeared in favor of the name *tennis,* anyway.) One of Wingfield's men took the game to Bermuda, where it was an instant hit. While on a visit to Bermuda, an American, Mary Outerbridge, saw a lawn tennis match and took the idea back to the United States. She even succeeded in getting a court built on Staten Island in New York City.

That was really the beginning of tennis in the United States. Today tennis is extremely popular. People of all ages and walks of life have discovered its appeal. With the invention of bubbles, which can instantly turn an outdoor court into an indoor one, the sport has become one of the nation's most popular year-round activities.

TRACK AND FIELD (ATHLETICS)

The ability to run comes naturally to men and women—and for very good reason. The leg muscles used to catch a departing bus or train or to run the 100-yard dash, or sprint, are the same ones our ancestors used thousands of years ago to get away from dangerous beasts.

Track and field may well be the sport with the most complete recorded history. Sports' historian John Kieran writes of a Greek man named Corobus winning "a great footrace in a meadow beside the river Alpheus at Olympia in 776 B.C." That was probably the very first Olympic athletic event.

According to ancient records, there was only one event in those first Olympic Games. It was a race known as the *stade* (our modern word *stadium* comes from this word) and was about 200 yards (182 meters) in distance—probably because that was the length of the arena. Fifty years later, a second event, the double stade, was added. At a still later date, a distance race of about three miles was added.

In 656 B.C., a broad jump (known in modern track as the long jump) was added to the program, and a man named Chronis of Sparta won with a very respectable leap of 23 feet, 1½ inches. Later, the hop, step, and jump event and the javelin throw were included in the list of events. The Greeks also threw a piece of metal called a *hateres,* which in time became the discus.

The Olympic Games were played many times in the years that

followed, but they were marred by quarreling, bribery, and gambling scandals. Around A.D. 400 the games were banned by Theodosius I, the Christian emperor of Rome, who felt they were becoming a public nuisance.

The Games were revived in Greece in 1896. These "modern Olympics," as they are known, include an event not originally done in Olympia—the marathon.

After their victory over the Persian army, the ancient Greeks were anxious to get the good news back to their elders in Athens. A soldier fresh from battle was chosen to carry the message on foot from Marathon, the scene of the battle, to Athens—a distance of 26 miles, 385 yards (42.20 kilometers). The runner put his weapons to one side and ran himself right into history. Staggering through the gates of Athens, the messenger gasped out, "Rejoice, we conquer," then dropped dead. No one clocked his time, but since it killed him, the pace must have been terrific. The marathon event is run in honor of this celebrated run. In it, the contestants must run 26 miles, 385 yards (42.20 kilometers).

Greek words form the roots of many terms in the track and field vocabulary of today, among them *stadium, marathon, javelin,* and *discus.* The javelin event can be traced back to Greek soldiers who in their spare time held contests to see who could throw his heavy spear the farthest. Likewise, history's first pole-vaulters may have been Greek infantrymen using these same spears to jump over hedges and stone walls and to clear narrow streams. In ancient Olympia, the discus thrower was perhaps the most respected man in the competition, actually a hero to citizens of the city, and was often given special privileges.

After the early Olympic Games were banned, very little track and field activity took place until the twelfth century, when the English revived the sport—strictly on an amateur basis. No records were kept until the first college meet, Oxford against Cambridge, in 1864. Two years later, there was a national meet in London. And two years after that, the first track meet in the United States took place at the New York Athletic Club in New York City.

Before 1860, each country kept its own records separately. Then, during the 1860s, records of important track and field competitions were first kept on an international scale. The best of these

Running may have been the first competitive sport. This vase at left, dating back to the 6th century B.C., depicts such a contest.

Below: running as a sport grew quite popular in England in the late 1800s

were considered as world marks. In 1864, the world record for the 100-yard dash was around 10.5 seconds, and the mile mark was 4.56 minutes. A hundred years later, those two marks were down to 9.1 seconds and 3.51 minutes, respectively.

The Olympic Games now include several dozen different sports, but the track and field events are the backbone of every Olympic competition. Not surprisingly, track and field athletes have always grabbed the Olympic headlines. Traditionally, the man who wins the 100-meter dash is considered the world's fastest human. One of the most famous of these winners was Jesse Owens, who was voted track athlete of the first half of the twentieth century. Dr. Roger Bannister, an Englishman, became a worldwide hero when he broke the four-minute mile in 1954. The mile record has been going down ever since.

In June of 1940, Cornelius Warmerdam became history's first fifteen-foot (4.57 meters) pole-vaulter. Warmerdam used the traditional bamboo pole to set his record. Later on, vaulters pushed the record higher with the help of other kinds of poles. Today, the springy fiberglass pole threatens to send vaulters soaring to over nineteen feet (5.79 meters).

In Olympic track and field, there are twenty-four events for men and fourteen for women, all based on meters. In countries not on the metric system, such as the United States, there are about eight additional events based on yards. All told, including special relays and indoor events such as the 60-yard dash, there are almost fifty different events in track and field.

One of the most demanding—and dramatic—of these events is the decathlon. Actually, the decathlon is a series of ten events that take place over a two-day period. The first day's events include the 100-meter run, long jump, shot put, high jump, and 400-meter run. On the second day, the decathlon athletes must compete in the 110-meter high hurdles, the discus throw, the pole vault, the javelin throw, and the grueling 1,500-meter run.

Bob Mathias, a member of the United States team, won the Olympic decathlon title in 1948 at the age of seventeen. Four years later, he repeated the win, to become the only man to this day ever to win back-to-back Olympic decathlon championships.

From time to time, attempts have been made to professionalize track and field. The marathon runners tried it for money at the turn of the century. Australia used to have sprint series for money in the 1930s and 1940s. Then, in the 1970s, a well-financed attempt to set up a pro track circuit was made, using big arenas like Madison Square Garden. Track and field, however, is unusual in that it rarely attracts fans in great numbers. Yet track fans often know more about their sport than do fans of other sports.

Track and field records are made to be broken—as are records in most other sports. Performances that were once considered unbeatable have long since been bettered. Improved training methods and better nutrition helped. So did better conditions during competition and improved equipment, the fiberglass vaulting pole, for instance. Also, modern athletes are bigger and faster than their grandparents. Will each generation continue to improve in skill? Probably. But only time will tell for sure.

VOLLEYBALL

Volleyball, like basketball, was invented at a YMCA in Massachusetts. William G. Morgan thought up the game while working as a Y director in Holyoke, Massachusetts, in 1895. He wanted a game that would appeal to older men. Morgan never dreamed his sport would one day be played by athletes of all ages in international and Olympic competition.

Volleyball was first called minonette. It was played indoors and used a lawn tennis net and the inflated rubber inner lining of a basketball.

As with most new games, minonette was slow to become popular. For a time it was played only at the Holyoke Y. But eventually its fans infected new players with their enthusiasm and the game caught on in nearby Springfield. It was in Springfield that a Dr. A. T. Halsted, while watching a game being played, suggested that its name be changed to volleyball, a name more clearly describing the action of the game.

Interest in volleyball now began to increase faster than new facilities could be built. So people began to make volleyball courts by stretching nets between trees and marking off boundaries.

High schools, colleges, and towns began to make volleyball courts available. By 1916, men who were playing regularly wrote a new set of rules, which soon came into general use.

The first volleyball tournament was held in 1922 under the direction of the Y. In 1928, the United States Volleyball Association was formed. Its purpose was to regulate competitive play.

Volleyball is a good sport for men and women who have had little exercise, and for children who are too young to have skills for more demanding sports. They can all enjoy a casual game of volleyball at a local club. Long training periods are not needed before one can play.

Volleyball can also be played as a very tough and competitive sport. One need only recall the controversial 1972 Olympic volleyball final. Casual it wasn't. Volleyball can involve a variety of skills, as shown by the hotly contested Olympic volleyball events.

Of course, at the net a tall player will always have an advantage over a small player. But the rules of volleyball call for rotation of the players after each service. Thus a given player is at net position only three times in six. In the back row, mobility is the key. The best players are those who move well. The player who is strong on the front line may not move fast enough to help the team when he or she leaves the net position.

A regulation volleyball court is sixty feet long and thirty feet wide (18.30 meters by 9.15 meters). A net eight feet (2.44 meters) high divides the court in half, which makes a square of each of the sides. These dimensions have not changed much over the years, but the strategy and skill of the players definitely have, and the tempo of the game has greatly increased since Morgan invented it in 1895.

WRESTLING

Wrestling is one of history's oldest sports. It began with the fighting for survival necessary in prehistoric times. It was well known as a sport long before records were kept on other forms of athletics.

We can see the sport of wrestling pictured on wall paintings found in the tombs of Beni Hasan, a village in Middle Egypt. These paintings show that five thousand years ago the Egyptians used just about every wrestling hold known today. There is evidence also that wrestling was an important sport for the ancient Greeks. We have actual printed records of wrestling results from the eighteenth Olympian Games, held in 708 B.C.

In ancient Greece, wrestlers were respected figures, second only to discus throwers in the public's esteem. The Greeks enjoyed a routine called the *pancratium.* This was a rough sport that combined boxing, wrestling, and brawling. Even gouging, biting, and strangling were permitted. Extra points were scored if one contestant broke the other fellow's knuckles. The ancient Greek poet Homer sang of such wrestling prowess in his account of a match between the ancient Greek champion Ulysses and the Trojan hero Ajax, in the *Iliad.*

The Romans put a stop to such roughness and developed their own brand of wrestling, known today as Greco-Roman wrestling. Milo of Croton is generally considered to be the greatest of the ancient Greco-Roman wrestlers. However, when the roughness of the wrestling bouts was eliminated, much of the thrill went out of watching them.

**Wrestlers depicted on the base of
an excavated ancient Greek wall**

Royalty were patrons of the sport of wrestling in the Middle Ages. Kings and princes supported stables of wrestlers, and frequently got into the action themselves.

Britain had several styles of wrestling, each named after a different area of the country. The Lancashire style was the forerunner of today's catch-as-catch-can wrestling. Its aim was to pin both shoulders of an opponent. Punishing holds such as the stranglehold, the hammerlock, and the toehold were banned.

A different type of wrestling, called *sumo,* developed in Japan. People were bred to this sport, with sumo wrestlers marrying daughters of other sumo wrestlers. Weight was highly prized. Wrestlers weighed, and still weigh, 350 to 400 pounds (158.76 to 181.44 kilograms), with almost all of it muscle. Sumo is very ceremonial. Wrestlers braid their hair and anoint their bodies with oil before a match. The Japanese also invented jujitsu and judo, other forms of wrestling. In these sports, the offensive effort of an opponent is turned against him or her, with devastating results. These two activities have caught the fancy of millions of young people everywhere.

When you think of Abraham Lincoln, do you think of him as a wrestler? Most people don't, but it's a fact that Lincoln was the greatest wrestler among the presidents of the United States. He never wrestled for much money, though.

At the turn of the century, professional wrestling grew very popular. Today pro wrestling isn't really a sport. Its gimmickry makes it more just entertainment. Things such as "masked marvels" and team matches have brought it a long way from the serious contests of the ancient peoples. Amateur wrestling, however, is definitely a sport. Competition at the high school and college levels is intense.

Weight classifications in wrestling are similar to those in boxing. The main difference is that in wrestling there are several classifications of weights over 175 pounds (79.38 kilograms), whereas all boxers of 175 pounds and over are classified as heavyweights.

**A Japanese
wrestling match**

INDEX

ABOUT THE AUTHORS

Don Smith is currently a sportswriter and senior editor in New York City. He has authored a number of books for educational use, including many on combining sports with other interests, such as ecology. Mr. Smith attended Columbia and New York University. He has been a language specialist for United States Naval Intelligence and was for twelve years director of public relations for the New York Football Giants.

Dr. Anne Marie Mueser is currently an associate professor of education at Teachers College, Columbia University. She was sports editor of her college newspaper and the first woman to be official scorekeeper for the varsity basketball and baseball teams there. Dr. Mueser has, in the past, authored a number of reading materials for children.